SUPER
STRUCTURES

Written by
PHILIP WILKINSON

Pont de Normandie over the Seine
River near Honfleur, France

Semi-
submersible
service
vessel

Headquarters of the Hongkong
and Shanghai Bank, Hong Kong

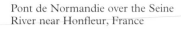

A DK PUBLISHING BOOK

Editor Laura Buller

Art editor Ann Cannings

Senior art editor Diane Klein

US editor Camela Decaire

Managing editor Gillian Denton

Managing art editor Julia Harris

Editorial consultant David J. Brown

Research Julie Ferris

Additional design Diane Clouting

Picture research Jo Carlill

Production Charlotte Traill

Photography Andy Crawford, Geoff Brightling
Modelmakers Alec Saunders and the team at
Thorp Modelmakers; Chris Reynolds and the team at
BBC Visual Effects; Gerry Judah

First American Edition, 1996
2 4 6 8 10 9 7 5 3 1

Published in the United States by
DK Publishing, Inc., 95 Madison Avenue,
New York, New York 10016
Visit us on the World Wide Web at http://www.dk.com

Copyright © 1996 Dorling Kindersley Limited, London

A CIP catalog record is available from the Library of Congress.

ISBN 0-7894-1011-7

Reproduced in Italy by G.R.B. Graphica, Verona
Printed in Singapore by Toppan

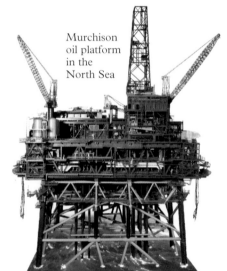

Triple tubes of the Channel
Tunnel, viewed from above

Murchison
oil platform
in the
North Sea

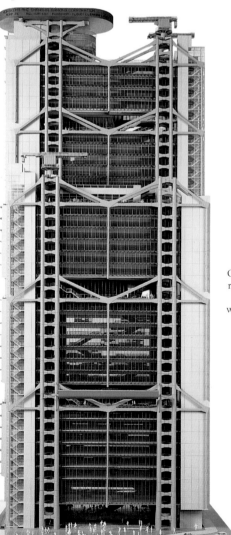

Triple-looped
roller coaster

Northbound, southbound, and service tunnels, Channel Tunnel

Contents

Steam generator inside a nuclear reactor

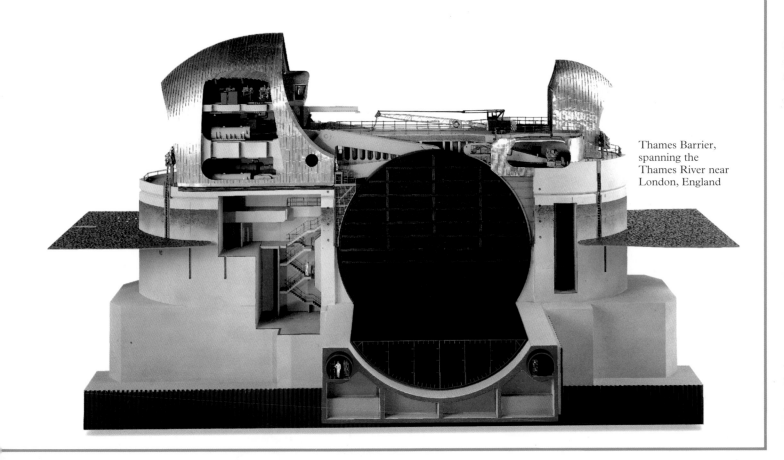

Thames Barrier, spanning the Thames River near London, England

Building a super structure

You are looking inside some of the world's most amazing buildings and other permanent structures in the pages of this book. All of them involved huge technological challenges – from designing a skyscraper able to withstand typhoon winds to ensuring safety in a tunnel under the sea – and hundreds of people. Architects and engineers created the designs, drew up the plans, and built models to show what each structure would look like, how it would be built – and just how it would work. Some of these models are featured in the following pages. During construction, teams of specialists worked on different parts of the structures, from driving foundation piles deep into the soil to fitting the cables of a bridge.

Drawing office
In this 19th-century architect's office, draftsmen sat on high stools, crouching over their drawings. Today, architects and civil engineers are more likely to sit in front of computer screens to draw up their building plans.

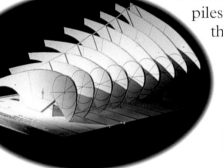

Working model
Many architects and engineers use models to help them figure out the shape of a building and its individual parts. This simple wood and cardboard model was made to help design the curving roof shape of the main terminal building at Japan's Kansai Airport (pp. 32-33).

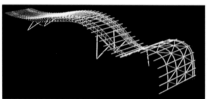

Computer model
Computer programs called CAD (computer-aided design) are useful tools for ironing out the details of complex structures, like the terminal roof at Kansai. CAD makes it easy to draw repeating elements, and to see the effects of changes quickly.

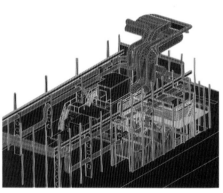

Invisible parts
Detailed drawings are made of the parts of a structure that will be hidden when it is finished. Most buildings, like this scientific laboratory, have services such as cables and ventilation ducts hidden within the floors and walls. CAD is used to determine where everything will go.

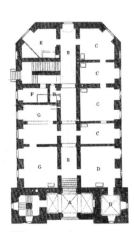

3-D model
A three-dimensional model of a structure and its site, like this one of the Inland Revenue Center at Nottingham, England, is often used to show how the building will look in its local surroundings.

Shallow blocks
The separate blocks of this building are shallow in plan, allowing natural light to reach all the offices.

Floor plan
Architects use floor plans like this one to give precise information about room sizes and the locations of windows, doors, and staircases. Floor plans can also show details from the positions of electrical sockets to the required building materials.

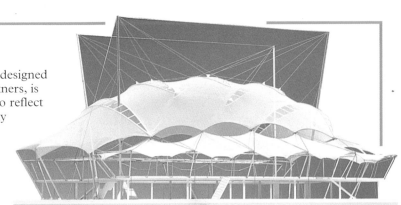

City within a city

The Inland Revenue Center, designed by Michael Hopkins and Partners, is laid out in a series of blocks to reflect the pattern of neighboring city streets. The offices do not have air conditioning; instead, the structure itself is designed to keep air moving.

Sports hall

The Inland Revenue Center has its own sports hall, with a tentlike fabric roof supported on steel poles. This model helped the architect and engineers plan and test its design.

Natural ventilation

This model of the Inland Revenue Center was made to show how its built-in ventilation system works.

Air outlets
Warm, stale air leaves the building through outlets at the tops of the towers.

Stair tower
Warm air rises up the glazed towers on the corner of each block.

Hot air
Sunlight heats up the air in the stair towers, making it rise.

Soffits
These reflect less dazzling light back into the offices.

Light shelf
This shades the area near the windows and reflects light up to the soffits (undersides of the arches).

Opening windows
Fresh air enters the building through open windows.

Vents
Floor-level vents also act as fresh-air intakes.

Skyscraper

Soaring towers of steel, glass, and concrete, skyscrapers are the ultimate structures. A skyscraper is a tall building in which the main weight of the structure is supported by a weatherproof, strong framework, as opposed to its outside walls. In many skyscrapers the framework is hidden away, and the building is covered with a skin of lightweight material. This is how some office towers manage to look as if made of glass. In the famous Hongkong Bank building, the steel framework of columns and beams supporting the skyscraper is visible on the outside.

Cross-braces
Pairs of masts are connected by two-story-high cross-braces, which give the structure extra strength.

Suspension trusses
Like giant coat hangers, pairs of suspension trusses join the masts to support the hangers.

Masts
Arranged in two rows of four, each mast is made of four columns of tubular steel, linked by horizontal beams.

Hangers support floor beams.

Floor beam

Hanging together
The structure of the bank is based on eight tall masts that are made up of a cluster of steel tubes, each joined to a series of rectangular cross-braces – like the rungs of a ladder. Huge diagonal beams, called trusses, connect the masts at five levels. Vertical beams, called hangers, run down from each truss. The 44 main floors are hung from these beams.

Column braced by short steel beams

Thinner at the top
The outer masts are shorter than the central pairs. This allows the building to "step back" at the top, so that it does not overshadow the street.

Double floors
Behind each huge truss is a two-story office floor.

Stairs
Glass-encased staircases run the full height of the building.

Cladding
The steel used on the outside of the building is covered in a close-fitting aluminum cladding to give it a smooth and protective finish.

Chicago fire
After a devastating fire in 1871, the city center of Chicago, Illinois, had to be rebuilt. Rising land prices made it cheaper to build up than to spread out, so architects hit on the idea of designing tall buildings in which the weight was supported by a metal framework – the first skyscrapers.

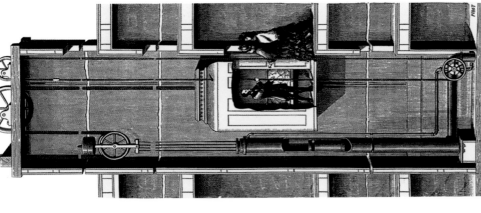

Continued on following page

Going up...

Tall buildings were not practical if you had to climb thousands of stairs to get to the top. Simple hoists had been around for centuries, but they were not safe for carrying people – if the cable broke, you could plummet to your death. In 1852 American engineer Elisha Graves Otis came up with a solution – the safety elevator. He developed a ratchet mechanism that "caught" the elevator if the cable broke.

Dangerous work

Many of the great American skyscrapers were built in the 1930s, before the introduction of modern safety precautions. Workers, nicknamed "skyboys," had little protection on scaffolding hundreds of feet high.

Catching the sun

The external sunscoop reflects natural light into the atrium.

The Hongkong Bank

Rising 46 stories above Hong Kong island, the Hongkong Bank building is one of the most innovative skyscrapers in the world. It was designed by British architect Sir Norman Foster and completed in 1985. Its unusual structure is visible from the outside, clearly showing how each floor hangs, suspended from a simple framework of metal.

Grand entrance

An open, two-story plaza facing a public square forms the entrance to the bank.

Instant rooms

The bank's restrooms were built as prefabricated, room-sized modules. Each is a steel box with a concrete floor, and was fully fitted with everything from toilets to soap dishes before being delivered to the building site and hoisted into place by cranes.

Diagram of typical restroom module

Sunscoop

The center of the bank is flooded with light – but it is all done with mirrors. A sunscoop, a panel of 24 toughened glass mirrors held on aluminum racks, hangs on the south side of the building. The mirrors, moved by computer-controlled electric motors, follow the path of the Sun and reflect light up to another sunscoop inside the building. This projects light into the atrium.

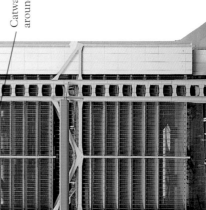

Crane cladding
The crane is clad to match the rest of the building.

Heavy load
This counterweight keeps the crane from toppling over.

Roof terraces on double-height floors are emergency exits.

Catwalks run around each level.

Helipad
A helicopter landing pad tops the building, but air traffic rules prevent its use.

Best view in town

A private elevator takes bank executives to an office suite, an observation gallery, a dining room, and a patio garden at the top of the building. The gallery offers a superb view over Hong Kong.

Maintenance crane

The skyscraper has its own built-in cranes, with long booms that can swing out over the glass facade. This allows windows to be cleaned and gives workers access to hard-to-reach parts of the exterior.

Stacked up

This view of the Hongkong Bank building reveals how this skyscraper works as a series of stacked zones – almost like separate "villages."

At the level of each of the diagonal trusses is a two-story public area where visitors can gather and meet.

People take high-speed elevators to one of these double-height floors, then take an escalator to any floor in between they require.

Glazed typhoon screen can be lowered to protect entrance plaza.

Open-plan offices

At night, the offices are visible through the glass walls. The outer areas of each floor are "open-plan," so that natural light can reach as many people as possible.

Void services

Underneath each floor is a space about 2 ft (60 cm) deep called a void. In this space are essential services for the floor above, including electrical, communications, and air-conditioning outlets. Voids also contain lighting and sprinkler equipment for the floor below, as well as smoke detectors and public address systems.

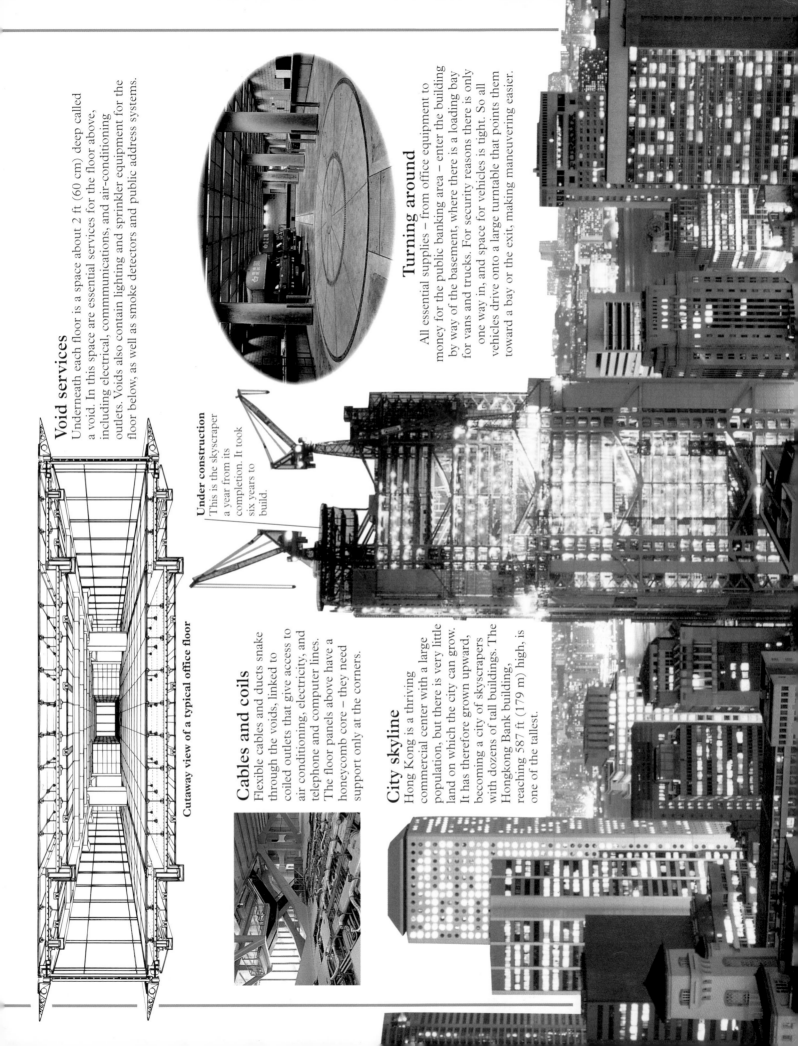

Cutaway view of a typical office floor

Under construction
This is the skyscraper a year from its completion. It took six years to build.

Turning around

All essential supplies – from office equipment to money for the public banking area – enter the building by way of the basement, where there is a loading bay for vans and trucks. For security reasons there is only one way in, and space for vehicles is tight. So all vehicles drive onto a large turntable that points them toward a bay or the exit, making maneuvering easier.

Cables and coils

Flexible cables and ducts snake through the voids, linked to coiled outlets that give access to air conditioning, electricity, and telephone and computer lines. The floor panels above have a honeycomb core – they need support only at the corners.

City skyline

Hong Kong is a thriving commercial center with a large population, but there is very little land on which the city can grow. It has therefore grown upward, becoming a city of skyscrapers with dozens of tall buildings. The Hongkong Bank building, reaching 587 ft (179 m) high, is one of the tallest.

On stage

From theater to ballet, opera to rock concerts, comedy to cabaret – the list of entertainments on offer in a modern city seems almost endless. But most cities cannot afford a separate building for each kind of event. In Cerritos, California, this problem was solved by creating a structure that is five buildings in one. The Cerritos Center for the Performing Arts, designed by Barton Myers Associates, uses modern technology to move almost 1 million pounds (0.5 million kg) of stage equipment – seats, floors, and ceilings – so that the interior of the auditorium can change according to the type of entertainment on offer, providing the audience with an exciting, ever-changing venue.

Seating towers
Movable, steel-framed seating towers line the side walls.

Layered seats
Tiers of seats ensure that everyone in the audience has a good view of the stage.

Pivots
These allow the side seating towers to rotate inward, away from the walls.

One building, one purpose
Traditional theaters are not very adaptable because the floors, stage, and seating are usually fixed in place. Some Renaissance theaters of the 16th century even had permanent scenery.

View from the stage
In this view, the theater is arranged for drama. Behind the floor seating are three semi-circular tiers of seats. Towers hold boxes on both sides of the theater.

On top
Flagpoles hung with bright banners top the roofs.

Entrance front
The Cerritos Center is highly decorated on the outside, with glass-enclosed elevators, hanging banners, and colorful geometric tilework. The walls are a mixture of polished red granite banded with limestone. Pyramid-shaped roofs top the towers and major sections of the arts complex.

Five theater floor plans viewed from above

Raising the floor
Sunken panels lift to level the floor space.

Seat storage
Seats are stored under the floor.

Cabaret
For banquets and cabaret performances the entire floor is leveled to provide a large area for dining tables and chairs. The boxes are used for additional seating.

Swinging seats
The towers move inward on air-filled casters that glide across the floor.

Fly tower for scenery

Stage
The wide, deep stage is ideal for operas and musicals with large casts.

Lyric
A 1,450-seat opera house can be created by sliding some of the seating towers behind the stage and lowering part of the floor to make an orchestra pit.

Take a seat

All but the tiered seats move to give everyone an excellent view of the performance. The towers contain small balconies that seat groups of eight or ten people.

Entrance lobby

The lobby is a spacious concrete structure joined to the auditorium at the tiered seating end. It provides access to each seating level, and plenty of room for the audience to circulate before shows and during intermissions.

View from the circle

The arena arrangement allows for seating all around the auditorium. The seats closest to the stage are moved into place on air casters.

Rear-stage seats
This seating unit weighs 225,000 lb (102,060 kg), yet it can be moved away on air casters when not in use.

Podium
Four elevators can raise or lower sections of the floor to provide a raised podium – or a flat surface.

Side stage seating units
Two of these seating units, each weighing 140,000 lb (63,504 kg), flank the central stage.

Angled arms
Tilting the arms brings the audience closer to the performers on stage.

Center stage
The stage is in the middle, surrounded by seating.

Stay seated
Seats in the tiered levels are the only ones in the theater that do not move.

Backstage seating
A raised platform behind the stage holds more seats.

Drama

Moving the stage forward from the lyric arrangement creates a more compact 900-seat theater. This is the right size for smaller-scale theatrical productions.

Arena

A raised podium stage and space enough for an audience of up to 1,780 people makes the arena arrangement ideal for sports events and rock concerts.

Concert

With a narrow central podium for the performers and seating boxes lining the walls, this arrangement provides a total of 1,936 seats – perfect for classical music concerts.

Big blue

With its vivid blue walls echoing the colors of the Mediterranean sea and sky, the regional government headquarters building of Marseille, France, is both a landmark and a symbol of the town. British architect William Alsop won a competition to design the building, known as *Le Grand Bleu* – the big blue. Its strong color and unusual shapes make a lasting impression, but it is also a functional design that reflects the structure's two main requirements – one building for council chambers and another for administration offices. Its design also meets the challenges of the local weather, which include strong winds that can cause damaging stresses to a building's structure and dazzling southern sun.

Inside the atrium
The central space, or atrium, is open to the public. It provides access to a restaurant, day-care center, library, information desk, and the offices themselves. At one end is the ovoid, a steel-framed, oval-shaped pod used for exhibitions.

Unpeeled
The skin of the building is pulled back to expose the riblike frame.

Walkways
The council building is wrapped with walkways.

Blue roof
A snakelike skin of blue triangular panels covers the council building roof.

What's inside?
Two council debating chambers, a function room, and a club are housed inside the council building.

Three into one
This view shows the building's three main parts: the curved airfoil structure sits on top of the tall administration section, with the tapering oval of the council section seen in front. A stretched fabric awning covers much of the council section's roof. This covering acts as a sun screen and also channels strong prevailing winds over the building.

In the shade
The walkway is shaded by the awning.

Steel rings of frame

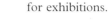

Awning anchors
These rods anchor the roof awning.

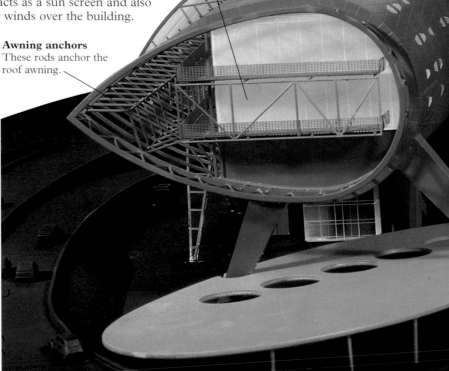

The council building
This building stands on seven pairs of splayed concrete legs that lift it above ground level. The legs support a riblike framework of tubular steel rings that are larger in the center and smaller at the ends, giving the building its distinctive curve.

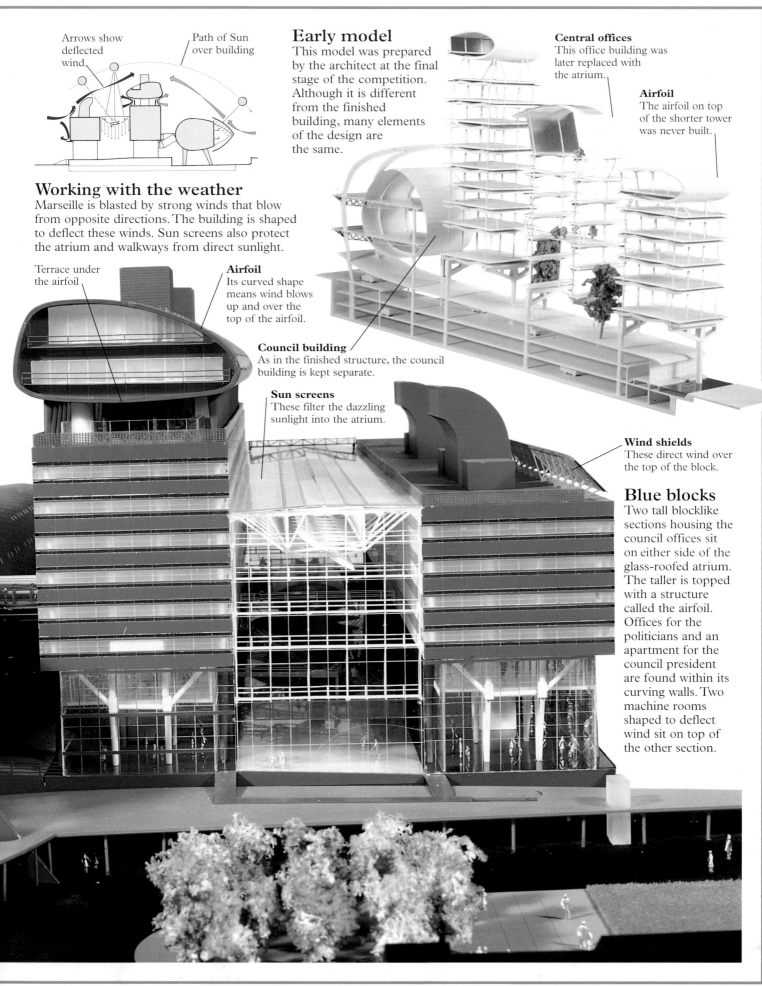

Arrows show deflected wind

Path of Sun over building

Early model

This model was prepared by the architect at the final stage of the competition. Although it is different from the finished building, many elements of the design are the same.

Central offices
This office building was later replaced with the atrium.

Airfoil
The airfoil on top of the shorter tower was never built.

Working with the weather

Marseille is blasted by strong winds that blow from opposite directions. The building is shaped to deflect these winds. Sun screens also protect the atrium and walkways from direct sunlight.

Terrace under the airfoil

Airfoil
Its curved shape means wind blows up and over the top of the airfoil.

Council building
As in the finished structure, the council building is kept separate.

Sun screens
These filter the dazzling sunlight into the atrium.

Wind shields
These direct wind over the top of the block.

Blue blocks

Two tall blocklike sections housing the council offices sit on either side of the glass-roofed atrium. The taller is topped with a structure called the airfoil. Offices for the politicians and an apartment for the council president are found within its curving walls. Two machine rooms shaped to deflect wind sit on top of the other section.

Beneath the streets

The veins and arteries of a modern city lie beneath its streets. Cables and pipes carry essential services such as electricity and gas; drains take away waste; subway trains rush through tunnels. In most cities, the spate of excavating and tunneling that provided all these services began in the nineteenth century, with hand-dug sewers. Many modern cables and pipes are still installed by hand, but engineers also use huge tunnel-boring machines. Work is constant – early pipes were made of clay or iron, and are now being replaced by longer-lasting concrete and plastic. New technologies provide a need for new underground networks as well. One of the most recent developments is fiber-optic cable, which can carry all kinds of information from television signals to computer data.

City of the dead

The ancient Romans sometimes buried their dead in vast networks of underground passages called catacombs. These, at Tyre, Lebanon, date from AD 200. The remains of the deceased were placed on shelves or their ashes were deposited in urns after cremation.

Road surface of crushed rock mixed with bitumen and sand

Mixed rocks such as limestone and granite make the road base.

Subsoil

The first sewers

Raw sewage once poured through open ditches. As cities grew, the sight and smell became so bad that vast sewage pipes were built. The first were dug by hand and lined with arching brick vaults. Many of these are still in use.

Slice through a city

Each section of this model shows one slice beneath a typical city street. Just below pavement level are the essential services needed by every house on the street – from drains to telephone lines. Lower down are underground train tunnels and the main sewers that serve large numbers of homes. Water supply tunnels are found at the lowest level, far beneath the surface.

Pumping water

Water is supplied to large cities through deep concrete tunnels. These can be up to 8 ft (2.5 m) wide – big enough to drive a car through. Huge electric pumps like these bring water up to the surface.

Twin tunnels
Concrete-lined tunnels carry water from treatment plants to an entire city.

Network of sewers carries waste into large main sewer.

Electric streetlights

Water from street runs through drains into sewer.

Each pair of wires in a telephone cable carries one call.

Fresh water supply

Computerized pig

Pipelines must be kept in good condition, but it is difficult to check a pipe for flaws once it is buried. Engineers send remote-controlled inspection units, nicknamed "pigs" due to their long, rounded shape, down pipelines to check them from the inside. Sensors around the pig pinpoint any defects, storing the data on a built-in computer. The data is collected and read when the pig finishes its run.

Cable for television and radio signals

Gas pipes have thick walls to prevent leaks.

Low-voltage electricity cable

High-voltage electricity cable

Modern main sewer lined with concrete rings

Safe under the streets

During World War II, German planes bombarded British cities at night in a campaign called the Blitz. Thousands of people sheltered, and even slept, on the station platforms of London's subway system. When an air-raid warning sounded, people ran down into the nearest station.

Subway tunnels
Underground trains run in deep tunnels excavated beneath building foundations.

Tunnels under the sea

Linking Britain with the rest of Europe for the first time since the frozen wastes of the last Ice Age covered the area, the Channel Tunnel is a spectacular engineering feat. The 31-mile (50.5-km) triple-tubed tunnel, of which 23 miles (38 km) are under the sea, took less than seven years to build. Enormous tunnel-boring machines pushed their way through about 247 million cu ft (7 million cu m) of rock, leaving completed sections of tunnel behind. Although the underwater tunnels are the heart of the system, the project also included three land tunnels, two terminals, and passenger, car shuttle, and freight trains.

Eurostar trains

Passengers without cars travel through the tunnel on high-speed Eurostar trains. Based on the design of the French TGV, the trains reach a maximum speed of 186 mph (300 km/h) – 100 mph (160 km/h) in the tunnel itself. A journey from London to Paris takes three hours; Brussels takes 15 minutes more.

Tunnel dreams

People have dreamed and schemed about a tunnel under the Channel for hundreds of years. This 1914 drawing shows one fanciful idea of how a tunnel might work.

Dumping ground

Much of the chalky rock dug from the tunnel ended up in this huge reservoir at Fond Pignon, France. Mixed with water into a yogurt-like slurry and pumped into the reservoir, the material set in a layer 131 ft (40 m) thick.

Emergency services

Specially built vehicles, equipped as fire engines, ambulances, or maintenance units, speed along the central service tunnel in an emergency. They can reach any part of the tunnel in 20 minutes.

Inside the tunnels

Each of the tunnels is packed with equipment – drainage, cooling and ventilation systems, electrical power supplies for the trains, lighting, computerized control systems, and railroad tracks. Equipment for maintaining all these systems is contained in the cross-passages and in the service vehicles that travel along the central tunnel.

A slice through the tunnel
The model shown below and on the next page shows a typical cross-section through the three underwater tunnels.

Electric cables

Drainage pipes

Fire-fighting equipment

Electricity supply
Some 808 miles (1,300 km) of electrical cable run along the tunnels, carrying power for lighting, signals, ventilation equipment, and the trains themselves.

Guidance system
Wires buried beneath the service tunnel floor guide the maintenance vehicles. The vehicles pick up signals from the wires so that they can be steered automatically.

Cooling water pipes

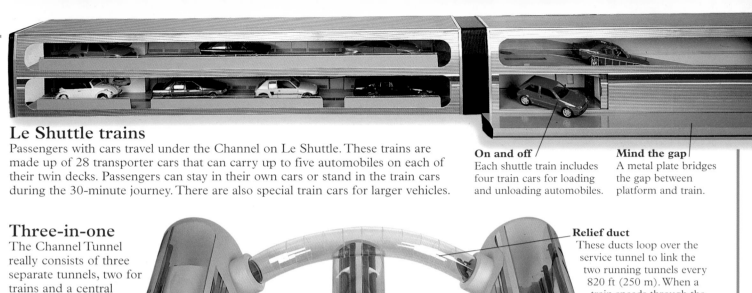

Le Shuttle trains

Passengers with cars travel under the Channel on Le Shuttle. These trains are made up of 28 transporter cars that can carry up to five automobiles on each of their twin decks. Passengers can stay in their own cars or stand in the train cars during the 30-minute journey. There are also special train cars for larger vehicles.

On and off
Each shuttle train includes four train cars for loading and unloading automobiles.

Mind the gap
A metal plate bridges the gap between platform and train.

Three-in-one

The Channel Tunnel really consists of three separate tunnels, two for trains and a central service tunnel for maintenance and emergency use. The three tunnels are connected every 1,230 ft (375 m) by cross-passages, which can be sealed off with massive metal bulkhead doors in case of fire.

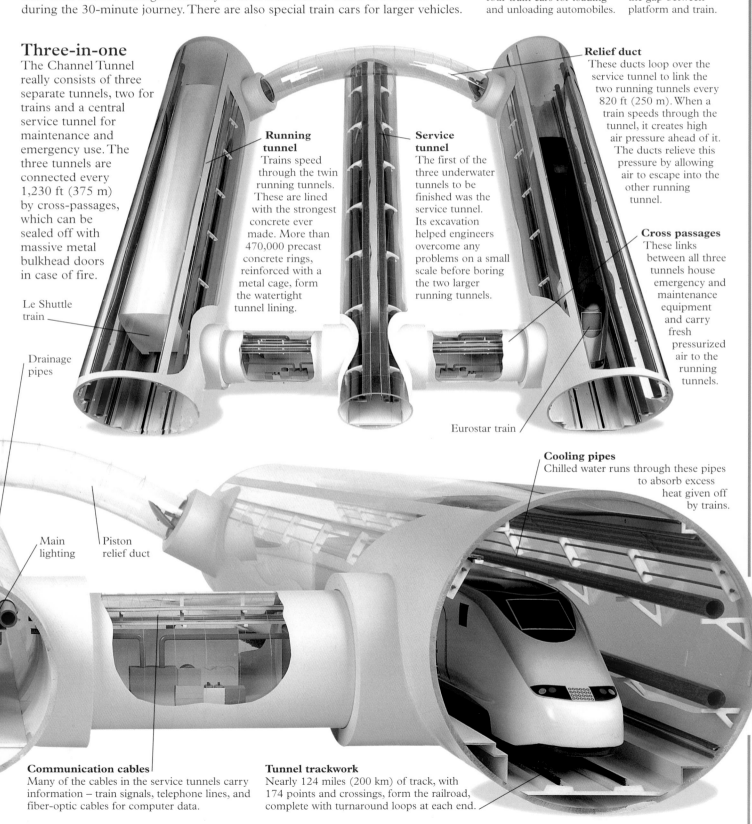

Le Shuttle train

Drainage pipes

Running tunnel
Trains speed through the twin running tunnels. These are lined with the strongest concrete ever made. More than 470,000 precast concrete rings, reinforced with a metal cage, form the watertight tunnel lining.

Service tunnel
The first of the three underwater tunnels to be finished was the service tunnel. Its excavation helped engineers overcome any problems on a small scale before boring the two larger running tunnels.

Relief duct
These ducts loop over the service tunnel to link the two running tunnels every 820 ft (250 m). When a train speeds through the tunnel, it creates high air pressure ahead of it. The ducts relieve this pressure by allowing air to escape into the other running tunnel.

Cross passages
These links between all three tunnels house emergency and maintenance equipment and carry fresh pressurized air to the running tunnels.

Eurostar train

Cooling pipes
Chilled water runs through these pipes to absorb excess heat given off by trains.

Main lighting

Piston relief duct

Communication cables
Many of the cables in the service tunnels carry information – train signals, telephone lines, and fiber-optic cables for computer data.

Tunnel trackwork
Nearly 124 miles (200 km) of track, with 174 points and crossings, form the railroad, complete with turnaround loops at each end.

Continued on following page

Cutting head
The head rotates as it pushes through the rock.

Operator's control cabin

Gripper shoes
These grip the rock and thrust the TBM steadily forward.

Chalky rock

Cutting head

At the end of each tunnel-boring machine (TBM) is an 880-ton (800-tonne) rotating cutting head (above) tipped with tough tungsten carbide picks for drilling rock.

Digging under the sea

The Channel Tunnel was cut with eleven giant TBMs. This is a model of one TBM and its backup services. Because it is so long, the TBM is shown from left to right, over four rows.

Crane
Lining segments are lifted with this crane and placed on a conveyer belt for delivery to the erectors.

Right track
Supply trains run along narrow-gauge railroad tracks right through the TBM backup.

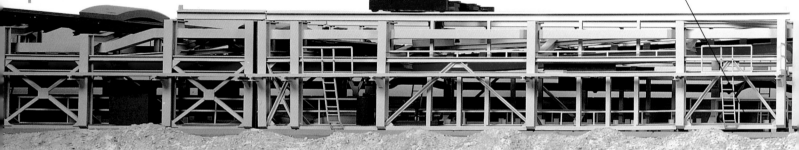

Ups and downs
Ladders connect each of the gantries of the TBM.

Adjustable belt
The conveyer can be extended to reach the right spoil wagon.

Spoil wagons
These wagons carry the excavated rock back to the tunnel entrance.

Conveyer discharge
The spoil pours off the conveyer belt into waiting wagons.

Meals on wheels
A cafeteria car – as well as an office, workshop, and restrooms – moves along with the TBM.

Ventilation duct
Fresh air is taken in through the main ventilation duct for circulation to the tunnel face.

Passenger car
The tunnel operators traveled to work on this train. Three shifts of 21 men worked around the clock.

Providing a push
This locomotive powers the supply train. Most trains were several hundred yards long.

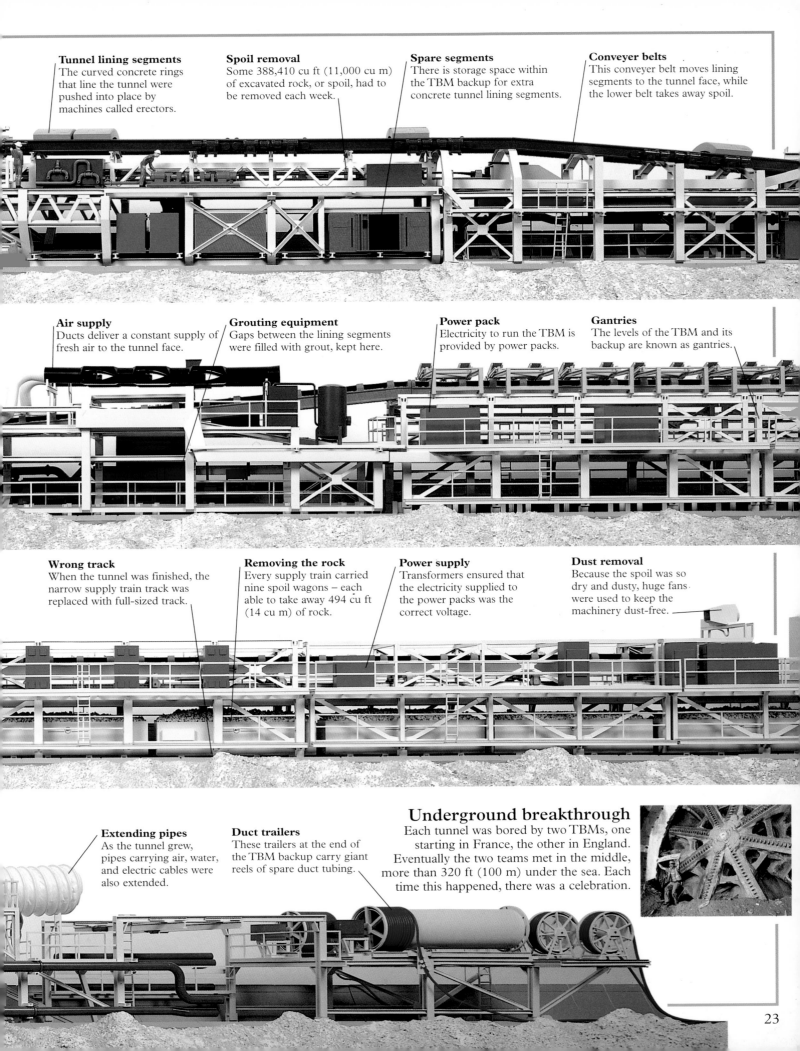

Tunnel lining segments
The curved concrete rings that line the tunnel were pushed into place by machines called erectors.

Spoil removal
Some 388,410 cu ft (11,000 cu m) of excavated rock, or spoil, had to be removed each week.

Spare segments
There is storage space within the TBM backup for extra concrete tunnel lining segments.

Conveyer belts
This conveyer belt moves lining segments to the tunnel face, while the lower belt takes away spoil.

Air supply
Ducts deliver a constant supply of fresh air to the tunnel face.

Grouting equipment
Gaps between the lining segments were filled with grout, kept here.

Power pack
Electricity to run the TBM is provided by power packs.

Gantries
The levels of the TBM and its backup are known as gantries.

Wrong track
When the tunnel was finished, the narrow supply train track was replaced with full-sized track.

Removing the rock
Every supply train carried nine spoil wagons – each able to take away 494 cu ft (14 cu m) of rock.

Power supply
Transformers ensured that the electricity supplied to the power packs was the correct voltage.

Dust removal
Because the spoil was so dry and dusty, huge fans were used to keep the machinery dust-free.

Extending pipes
As the tunnel grew, pipes carrying air, water, and electric cables were also extended.

Duct trailers
These trailers at the end of the TBM backup carry giant reels of spare duct tubing.

Underground breakthrough

Each tunnel was bored by two TBMs, one starting in France, the other in England. Eventually the two teams met in the middle, more than 320 ft (100 m) under the sea. Each time this happened, there was a celebration.

Grand span

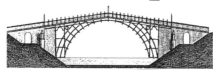

Ever since our prehistoric ancestors threw a log across a stream to get from one side to the other, people have built bridges. Engineers have devised several types of bridges, from the elegant arched bridges of the Romans, to the beautiful suspension bridges of the 19th and 20th centuries. A bridge must be strong enough to support its own weight – and the weight of the vehicles crossing it. The difference between the main types of bridges is in the way the forces exerted by these weights are displaced. Bridges must also withstand the forces of nature, from strong winds and freezing temperatures to earthquakes. France's Pont de Normandie, featured on the following pages, meets all these demands.

Beam bridge

The first bridge was probably a simple beam bridge, made by putting a plank across a stream. To span a wider distance, piers could be built up from the riverbed to support a few beams, end to end. Some ancient stone beam bridges still survive, like this one in Dartmoor, England. Both its piers and beams are made of hard, long-lasting granite.

Built to last

The world's first iron bridge was built across the Severn River at Coalbrookdale, England, in 1779. The town already had a booming iron industry – the first cast-iron railroad lines were made there – so iron, with its high tensile strength, was an obvious choice for the bridge. Most bridges built in the following century were of cast or wrought iron.

A deadly collapse

This rail bridge over the Tay River in Scotland, built in 1878, was an impressive structure some 2 miles (3.2 km) long, but the girders of the central spans were not securely joined to the others. The bridge collapsed during a gale on December 29, 1879, killing 75 passengers on a train crossing the bridge.

Cables connect directly to towering pylons; in a suspension bridge, most cables connect to other cables.

Cable-stayed bridge

The Pont de Normandie is a cable-stayed bridge. In this type of design, cables bear the weight of the roadway and transfer it to the pylons and the access viaducts on either side. This means that the loads of the central roadway and access viaducts balance each other, similar to a person carrying a suitcase in each hand.

Roadway
Two lanes of traffic cross the bridge in each direction.

Arch bridge
This type of bridge is used to cross a wide span where it is difficult to build supporting piers. The arch transfers the downward-pressing load into the ground at either end of the bridge.

Cantilever bridge
In this bridge, arms extend outward from central supports. Because it can cross a long span and can be made stiff and strong, it is ideal for heavy loads.

Suspension bridge
Another way of bridging a large gap is to hang the roadway from cables that pass over tall towers to anchor points at either end. This is called a suspension bridge.

Forth Rail Bridge
This large cantilever bridge in Scotland was designed by Sir John Fowler and Benjamin Baker and finished in 1889. In all it is about 1.5 miles (2.5 km) long, with steel cantilevers supporting two main spans 151 ft (46 m) above the waters of the Firth of Forth. The total weight of steel in the bridge is some 64,000 tons (58,000 tonnes).

Tyne Bridge
One of several bridges over the Tyne River in Newcastle, England, this bridge is of a steel arch design, with the roadway suspended from the arch by a rigid network of steel girders. The towers at either end act as weights, holding down the outward thrust of the arch.

Pylons
Each concrete pylon is shaped like an upside-down Y.

Mackinac Bridge
Though its central span is shorter than others, the very long side spans of the Mackinac suspension bridge in Michigan made it overall the world's longest at 1.6 miles (2.6 km) when it opened in 1957.

Super span
From pylon to pylon, the central span is 2,808 ft (856 m) long.

Pylon anchors 23 pairs of cables.

Across the waters
The Pont de Normandie crosses the estuary of the Seine River.

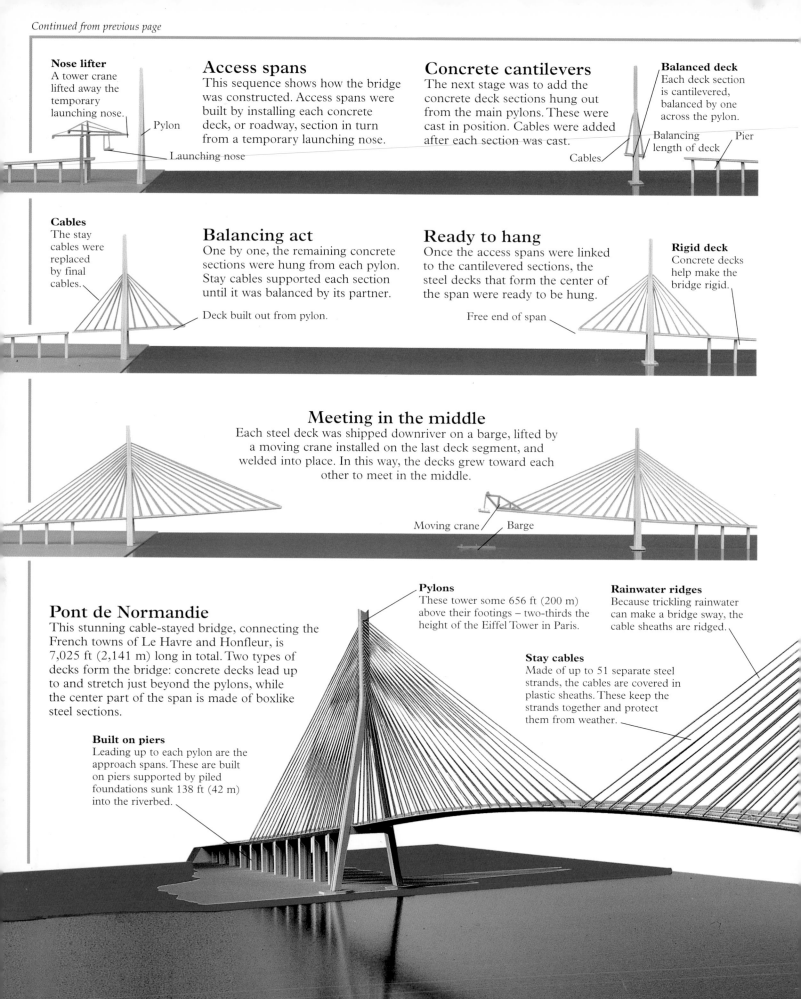

Nose lifter
A tower crane lifted away the temporary launching nose.

Pylon

Launching nose

Access spans
This sequence shows how the bridge was constructed. Access spans were built by installing each concrete deck, or roadway, section in turn from a temporary launching nose.

Concrete cantilevers
The next stage was to add the concrete deck sections hung out from the main pylons. These were cast in position. Cables were added after each section was cast.

Balanced deck
Each deck section is cantilevered, balanced by one across the pylon.

Cables

Balancing length of deck

Pier

Cables
The stay cables were replaced by final cables.

Balancing act
One by one, the remaining concrete sections were hung from each pylon. Stay cables supported each section until it was balanced by its partner.

Deck built out from pylon.

Ready to hang
Once the access spans were linked to the cantilevered sections, the steel decks that form the center of the span were ready to be hung.

Free end of span

Rigid deck
Concrete decks help make the bridge rigid.

Meeting in the middle
Each steel deck was shipped downriver on a barge, lifted by a moving crane installed on the last deck segment, and welded into place. In this way, the decks grew toward each other to meet in the middle.

Moving crane

Barge

Pont de Normandie
This stunning cable-stayed bridge, connecting the French towns of Le Havre and Honfleur, is 7,025 ft (2,141 m) long in total. Two types of decks form the bridge: concrete decks lead up to and stretch just beyond the pylons, while the center part of the span is made of boxlike steel sections.

Pylons
These tower some 656 ft (200 m) above their footings – two-thirds the height of the Eiffel Tower in Paris.

Rainwater ridges
Because trickling rainwater can make a bridge sway, the cable sheaths are ridged.

Stay cables
Made of up to 51 separate steel strands, the cables are covered in plastic sheaths. These keep the strands together and protect them from weather.

Built on piers
Leading up to each pylon are the approach spans. These are built on piers supported by piled foundations sunk 138 ft (42 m) into the riverbed.

Protecting the pylon

Base of pylon

Concrete-filled cofferdam

Riverbed layers
The pylon supports are sunk into layers of sand, clay, and limestone.

Piles supporting pylon

Because the northern pylon of the bridge sits in the river, it had to be protected from possible collisions with ships. A ring of cofferdams filled with concrete surrounds the footings of the pylon.

Anchorage boxes
Cables are attached to anchorage boxes on the upper sections of the pylons.

Damper cables

Bridge engineers had to ensure that the cables would not sway into each other in high winds. So damper cables, which hang at right angles to the main cables, were fitted to reduce possible movement.

Cable pairs
The cables are anchored in pairs, one on each side of the deck.

Lifting the deck into place

A mobile crane lifted each section of the deck to within 20 in (50 cm) of its correct position, and then eased it into place and welded it to its neighbors. Finally, each section's cables were installed, and the crane could release its grip.

Cable anchor point

Roadway

Cross-members stiffen deck

Ridges add strength

Deck section

With a streamlined shape designed to resist wind forces, the lightweight steel deck sections are built like empty boxes. Ridges running along the length of the deck and cross-members running across the width make it more rigid.

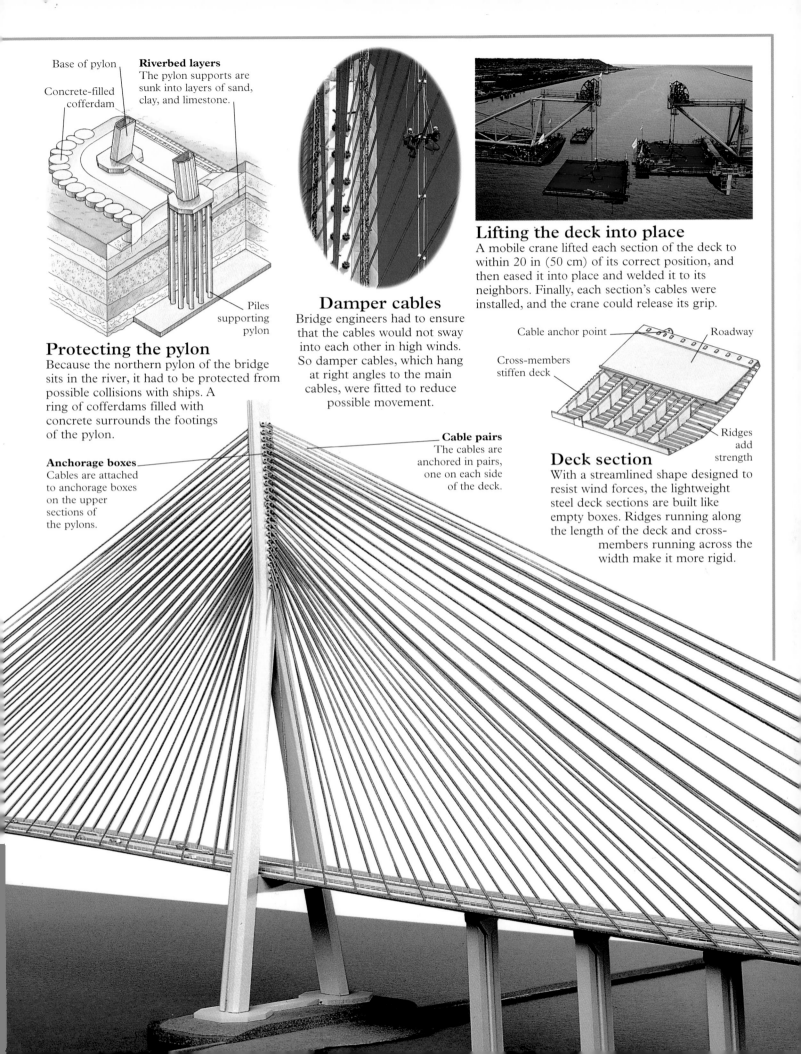

Taming the tides

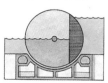

Ever since the Romans founded Londinium on the banks of the Thames River, it has been prone to sudden floods. The biggest menace comes from surge tides that periodically sweep across the North Sea, raising the sea level by 1 ft (300 mm) and pushing water up the Thames toward London at speeds of up to 60 mph (96 km/h). After several disastrous floods earlier this century, the English government decided to build a barrier across the river. The Thames Barrier consists of a series of gates, built between massive piers, that can be opened to let ships pass, and closed when there is a likelihood of flooding.

A city submerged
In 1953, the Thames spilled over its banks east of London. More than 300 people lost their lives, damage to buildings cost millions, and 160,000 acres (65,000 hectares) of farmland were swamped by saltwater.

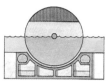

Open position

Flood control position

Maintenance position

Turning gates
Each of the barrier's gates can close to form a wall five stories high in just 20 minutes. The gates are raised to the top for maintenance.

Inside the barrier
Under the curving pier roofs are powerful hydraulic mechanisms that move the gates. Between the piers are the gates themselves. Those nearest the riverbanks are lifted above or lowered into the water. The gates in the center swing beneath the water when they are opened.

Rocking rams
A pair of hydraulic rams inside each pier push and pull to raise the rocker beams.

Steel shells
Each pier roof is a curving shell made of triple-layered timber covered with a protective skin of stainless steel strips.

Access tunnel
Linking the sills are two service tunnels big enough for engineers to walk through. These carry power cables, control cables, and drains, and provide access to all parts of the barrier.

Concrete cradle
The central gates are cradled in huge, curving concrete sills. These massive structures – the largest weighs 11,023 tons (10,000 tonnes) – were built on the riverbank. Tugboats towed them out to the piers, where they were flooded and sunk to the riverbed so that the gates could be built onto them.

Cofferdams

Before the barrier could be built, engineers had to construct cofferdams. These are submerged steel boxes from inside which the water is pumped to provide a dry building site. They were made by driving piles up to 78 ft (24 m) deep into the riverbed. The piers were built inside the cofferdams.

Gate arm
The gate arm rotates around a central shaft like a wheel on an axle. Each arm is loaded with steel to help counterbalance the weight of the gate. Wooden strips crisscross the arm, protecting it from impact by passing ships.

Maintenance crane
Each pier is topped with a crane for machinery maintenance.

Central pier
Sunk some 52 ft (16 m) into the solid chalk riverbed, the central piers are 36 ft (11 m) wide and 213 ft (65 m) long. Navigation lights at each end tell ships whether the gates are open or shut.

Rocker beams
Pairs of reversible hydraulic rams – one pulling and one pushing – move huge mechanical arms called rocker beams. The tips of the beams are connected to the gate arm, so that when the rocker beams move, the gate is lifted or lowered into position. This is quite a job – each gate weighs a massive 4,079 tons (3,700 tonnes).

Shift and latch
When the gate has been moved to its required position it is vital that it be held there. The shift and latch mechanism acts like an enormous bolt, locking the gate closed so that the pressure of a surge tide cannot force it open.

Elevator
An elevator links the top of the pier with the service tunnels.

Barrier gates
Plated with high-strength steel, the gates are made of hollow cells. They are protected from corrosion by 44 tons (40 tonnes) of paint.

Gap in the gate
A small space between the gate and sill always lets some water through to keep the river flowing.

Access tunnel

Sand ballast

Steel piles
These piles are the edge of the cofferdam inside of which the pier was built.

Across the river
From bank to bank, the barrier is about 1,706 ft (520 m) wide. Each of its four central openings spans 200 ft (61 m) – wide enough for ships to pass through. Weather conditions and tide levels are monitored at the barrier control center, enabling staff to decide when to close the gates. So far, the gates have been closed more than twenty times.

Loop the loop

Coaster disaster
Early roller coasters provided thrills – and spills. This engraving shows a man thrown to his death from a roller coaster car at Saint-Cloud, France, in 1891. Modern coasters have padded steel safety bars that hinge over the shoulders of each passenger, pinning them in place until the end of the ride.

After an agonizingly slow haul to the top of a steep slope, a roller coaster is allowed to hurtle down its tracks, picking up speed as gravity pulls the cars downhill. As the coaster climbs to take its first loop, its riders feel sheer exhilaration. The cars shoot upward, apparently defying gravity to hang briefly in midair at the top of the loop. Then they hurtle down again – but there's another stomach-churning loop just ahead. This mixture of fear and anticipation is probably what makes roller coasters so popular at today's amusement parks. The engineer's job is to make sure the ride is terrifying – yet also perfectly safe. Modern roller coasters have many safety features built in, from strengthened supports for the framework to specially designed brakes for the cars.

Heavy metal
The framework of a coaster this size contains about 2,755 tons (2,500 tonnes) of steel.

Momentum gained from the loops will push the coaster up the slope.

Heels over heads
On the Nemesis ride at England's Alton Towers theme park, the cars are suspended from the track, leaving the riders' feet dangling in midair. The idea is to make the passengers feel even less secure than on a traditional roller coaster – but the design is entirely safe.

Side braces for looping section of coaster

Tubes and ties
Roller coaster cars speed on air-filled tires over their steel path. The twin parallel tubes are secured to steel ties.

Wooden coaster
The first roller coasters were built of wood, and many new coasters are built in the same way. With its framework reinforced by cross-members, a wooden structure can be just as safe as a steel one, and enthusiasts claim that wood's slight flexing movement adds to the thrill of the ride.

Thick, tubular steel frame supports the rising track.

Steel roller coaster
Modern steel roller coasters often have one or more upside-down loops in addition to the steep up-and-down slopes of older coasters. This one turns its riders head over heels three times in all. It runs on a track made of steel tubes that reaches a height of almost 49 ft (15 m) at the tops of the loops. As they race around, the cars reach a top speed of about 60 mph (100 km/h).

Track attachment

Roller coaster cars run on wheels like railroad cars, but various safety devices stop them from falling off the track, or rolling backward down a hill if the chain that carries them up it fails. In this design, a second set of wheels can grip the track for added security.

Air-filled tires for smooth ride

Steel framework

The tubular steel framework that supports the raised section of the roller coaster is strengthened with diagonal braces that cross between each upright and horizontal beam.

Pinned to the track
At the top of the loop the cars are pushed against the track by centripetal force, which keeps a rotating object moving in a circle.

Steel safety bars keep riders in their seats.

Steel tubes brace the structure from the side.

Teardrop loop
The curve in a looping coaster is not a full circle, but a teardrop shape. This kind of loop creates more centripetal force at a slower speed, keeping passengers thrilled – but safe.

Coloring a coaster
It takes thousands of gallons of paint to color a coaster. A roller coaster of this size requires enough paint to cover more than five soccer fields.

Strong supports
Thick steel tubes shaped like inverted letter Vs are sunk on deep foundations to provide firm support for the coaster track.

Super airport

Air travel brings the world closer together – jets carry people and cargo between major cities in just a few hours. Air travel's increasing popularity has led to a need for larger airports that can operate 24 hours a day. But a busy airport operating all night disturbs local people and pollutes the atmosphere. One amazing airport provides a solution: Kansai International Airport is built on its own artificial island, about 3 miles (5 km) away from the shore of Honshu, Japan's main island. The terminal had to be made strong enough – and flexible enough – to withstand earthquakes and typhoon winds. It also had to be large enough to accommodate some 25 million passengers a year. To meet these demands, Italian architect Renzo Piano designed a vast building 1 mile (1,660 m) long, with an elegant, curving roof.

An artificial island
Kansai stands on an artificial island about 2.8 miles (4.5 km) long and 1.5 miles (2.5 km) wide in Osaka Bay. The island was made by building a rectangular sea wall around the edge of the site and then filling in the area in the middle. A six-lane highway, a railroad, and high-speed ferries provide access to the island.

Roof trusses
Made of tubular steel, the passenger terminal's striking triangular roof trusses rest on splayed support legs. They are designed to be rigid under normal conditions, but are flexible enough to bend without breaking in an earthquake. The white "sails" between the trusses are open ventilation ducts that send fresh air through the terminal.

Cladding
The curving roof of the terminal building is clad, or covered, with stainless steel panels. These are designed to resist corrosion from salt and pollution in the air. The side walls are made of large sheets of glass so that the terminal is flooded with sunlight.

Ins and outs
Passengers arrive at the terminal on the lower level and depart on the upper level.

Canyon
This four-story reception area provides access to each level of the terminal.

Floors for flights
Each floor of the terminal serves a different purpose, with domestic departures and arrivals sandwiched between the international floors.

Curving roof truss

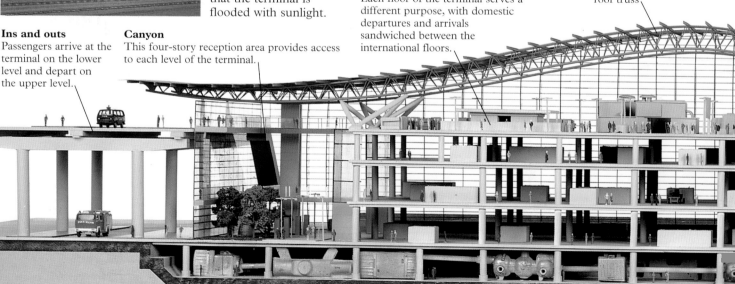

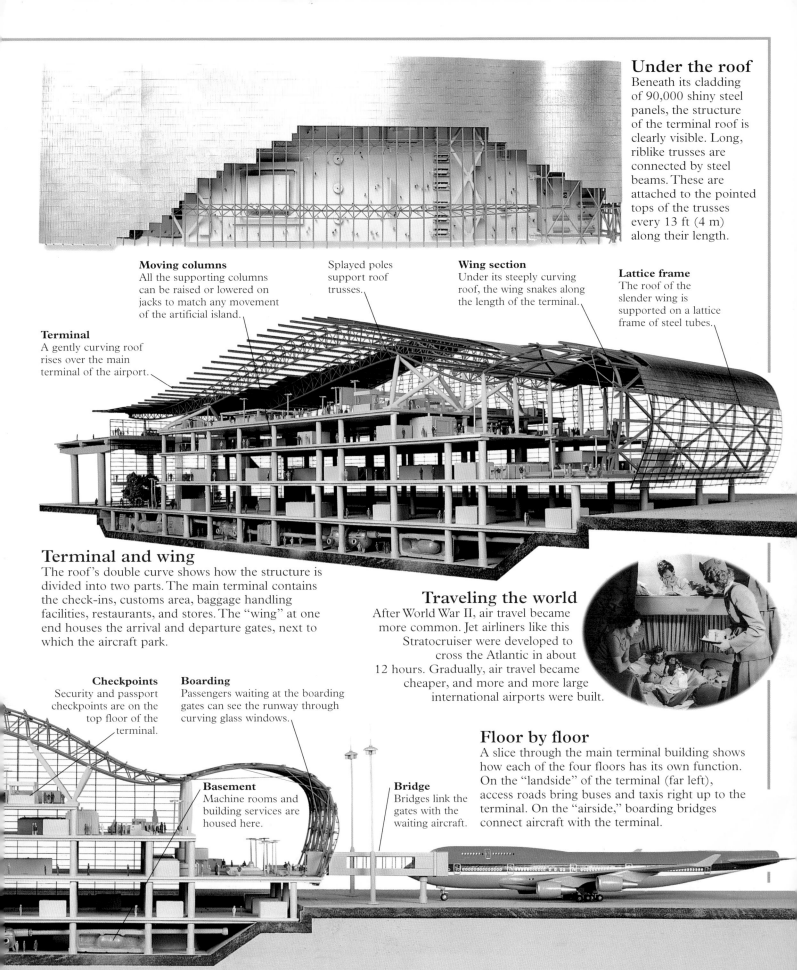

Under the roof
Beneath its cladding of 90,000 shiny steel panels, the structure of the terminal roof is clearly visible. Long, riblike trusses are connected by steel beams. These are attached to the pointed tops of the trusses every 13 ft (4 m) along their length.

Moving columns
All the supporting columns can be raised or lowered on jacks to match any movement of the artificial island.

Splayed poles support roof trusses.

Wing section
Under its steeply curving roof, the wing snakes along the length of the terminal.

Lattice frame
The roof of the slender wing is supported on a lattice frame of steel tubes.

Terminal
A gently curving roof rises over the main terminal of the airport.

Terminal and wing
The roof's double curve shows how the structure is divided into two parts. The main terminal contains the check-ins, customs area, baggage handling facilities, restaurants, and stores. The "wing" at one end houses the arrival and departure gates, next to which the aircraft park.

Traveling the world
After World War II, air travel became more common. Jet airliners like this Stratocruiser were developed to cross the Atlantic in about 12 hours. Gradually, air travel became cheaper, and more and more large international airports were built.

Floor by floor
A slice through the main terminal building shows how each of the four floors has its own function. On the "landside" of the terminal (far left), access roads bring buses and taxis right up to the terminal. On the "airside," boarding bridges connect aircraft with the terminal.

Checkpoints
Security and passport checkpoints are on the top floor of the terminal.

Boarding
Passengers waiting at the boarding gates can see the runway through curving glass windows.

Basement
Machine rooms and building services are housed here.

Bridge
Bridges link the gates with the waiting aircraft.

Stacked up

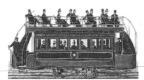

Bangkok, Thailand, is one of the most congested cities in the world – its population has doubled over the last 30 years. Because there is little public transportation, most people drive their own cars, creating terrible traffic jams. There are railroads at ground level, but the many road and rail crossings simply bring cars to a stop. The solution is to raise both trains and major roads above the ground. This is the idea behind BERTS – the Bangkok Elevated Road and Train System. On completion, BERTS will bring trains and vehicles 33 miles (53 km) from Rangsit in the north and Huamac in the east right into the center of Bangkok. To avoid creating even more traffic problems during construction, engineers designed concrete sections for BERTS that could could be manufactured off-site and assembled quickly over existing railroad tracks.

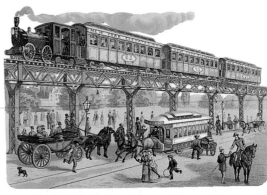

Raising the railroad
The idea of running a railroad on overhead tracks to ease street congestion is an old one. Many early city systems, like this one built in New York City in the 1880s, were raised up on tall viaducts to clear space below. People – and horsedrawn carriages – could pass through the spaces underneath.

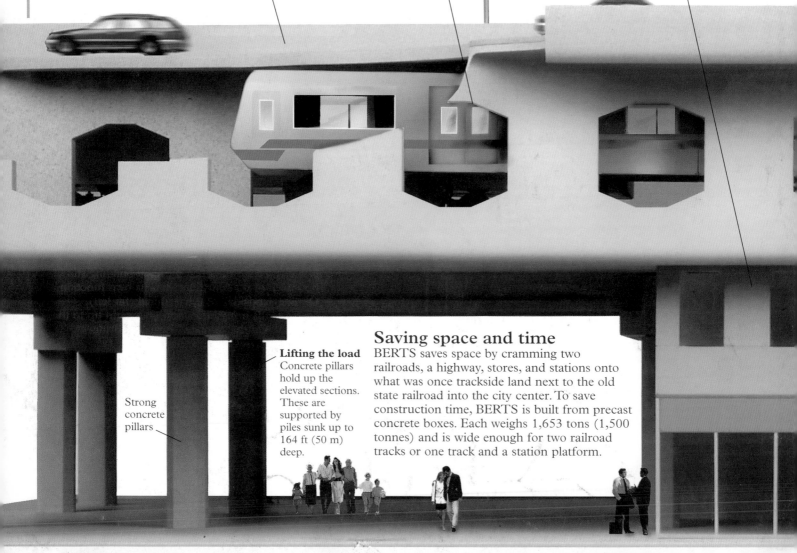

Six-lane highway
The elevated highway on top of BERTS has three lanes in each direction to ease traffic congestion.

Windows
Cut into the concrete walls, window openings provide ventilation for the railroad – and a view of the city.

Stores and offices
Raising the roads and rails creates space for stores and offices. There are plans to develop hotels and offices at major stations.

Strong concrete pillars

Lifting the load
Concrete pillars hold up the elevated sections. These are supported by piles sunk up to 164 ft (50 m) deep.

Saving space and time
BERTS saves space by cramming two railroads, a highway, stores, and stations onto what was once trackside land next to the old state railroad into the city center. To save construction time, BERTS is built from precast concrete boxes. Each weighs 1,653 tons (1,500 tonnes) and is wide enough for two railroad tracks or one track and a station platform.

High highways
Most modern highways have elevated sections and access ramps raised on columns. When two roads meet, this creates a complex pattern of roads on different levels, as seen here in Atlanta, Georgia.

Gridlock
When Bangkok's traffic grinds to a halt, people have little choice but to turn off their car engines and wait – or get out and walk. The city's traffic planners hope that BERTS will ease congestion and cut travel times.

State railroad
This rail network connects Bangkok with other cities throughout Thailand.

Local railroad
Up to three million passengers a day will use the commuter trains.

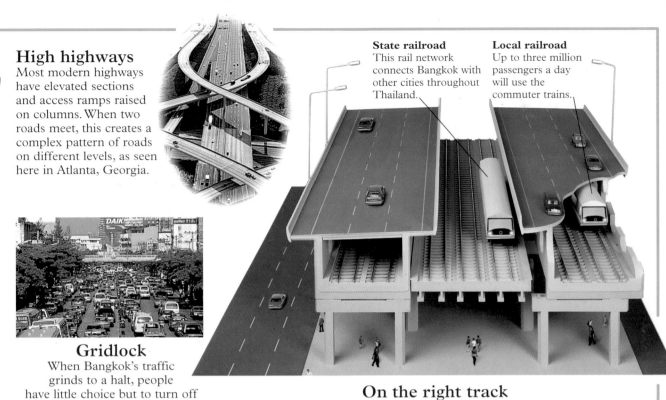

On the right track
The triple tracks of the state railroad run in the center of the structure, while commuter trains travel along each side. At street level, local roads will run beside the elevated system, giving access to the elevated highway and the stores and offices.

Stores at street level

Atom power

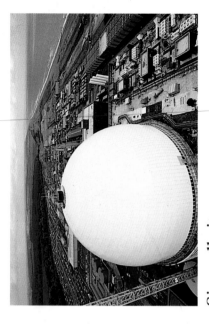

At the heart of a nuclear reactor like Sizewell B, tiny atoms of uranium are split to unleash a force able to match the heat and light of the Sun – and turn on ten million lightbulbs. Nuclear power stations capture this heat to boil water, creating jets of steam that drive huge turbines to produce electricity. Because the power of a nuclear reaction is so great – and potentially so dangerous – it has to take place inside an incredibly strong container called a pressure vessel. This is housed in a vast domed tower of concrete and steel, designed to keep in any radioactive material in the event of a leak, and to withstand any external dangers, from an earthquake to a plane crash.

Sizewell site

This aerial view shows the complex of buildings that make up the power station – everything from turbine houses to fuel storage areas and workshops. The power station is close to the coast because cold sea water is used to cool down the exhaust steam from the turbines, turning it back to water to be pumped back to the steam generator for reuse.

Safety suits

There are no workers in the containment building – because the high radiation levels are so dangerous, operators control the reactions from a separate building. But workers do sometimes handle radioactive material, such as used fuel rods. They must wear protective body suits like this one to limit the risk.

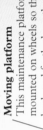

Breathe in
The suit must be airtight, so an oxygen pack gives fresh air.

Roman dome

The ancient Romans built domes to cover a large area with a strong roof without supporting pillars. Their biggest dome tops the Pantheon, a temple in Rome. Its diameter is about the same as that of the Sizewell B containment building.

Fuel assembly

The fuel that powers the nuclear reactions is held inside tall towers called fuel assemblies. Each contains 264 fuel rods, metal tubes filled with stacked pellets of radioactive uranium. These are lined up in rows with control rods between them. When the control rods are lowered toward the fuel rods, the reactions slow down; when they are lifted away, the reactions speed up again.

Control cluster
The control rods are clustered together to make them easier to lift and lower.

Huge steel frames hold the rods in place.

Fuel rods

Control rods

Containment building

At 210 ft (64 m) tall and 150 ft (45.7 m) wide, the massive containment building houses and protects the parts of the reactor: the pressure vessel, four steam generators, a coolant pump to circulate water around the core, and a pressurizer to keep this water under pressure. To give it strength, the building is made of a double layer of specially reinforced concrete wrapped around a tough framework of steel. Thick concrete also lines the base of the building and surrounds the pressure vessel.

Maintenance crane
A crane stretches across the containment building, allowing access to the equipment below.

Inner wall
The immensely strong inner wall is made of reinforced concrete 4 ft (1.3 m) thick. To stop any dangerous gases from escaping from the building, it is lined with a steel skin.

Moving platform
This maintenance platform is mounted on wheels so that it can roll back and forth along the crane.

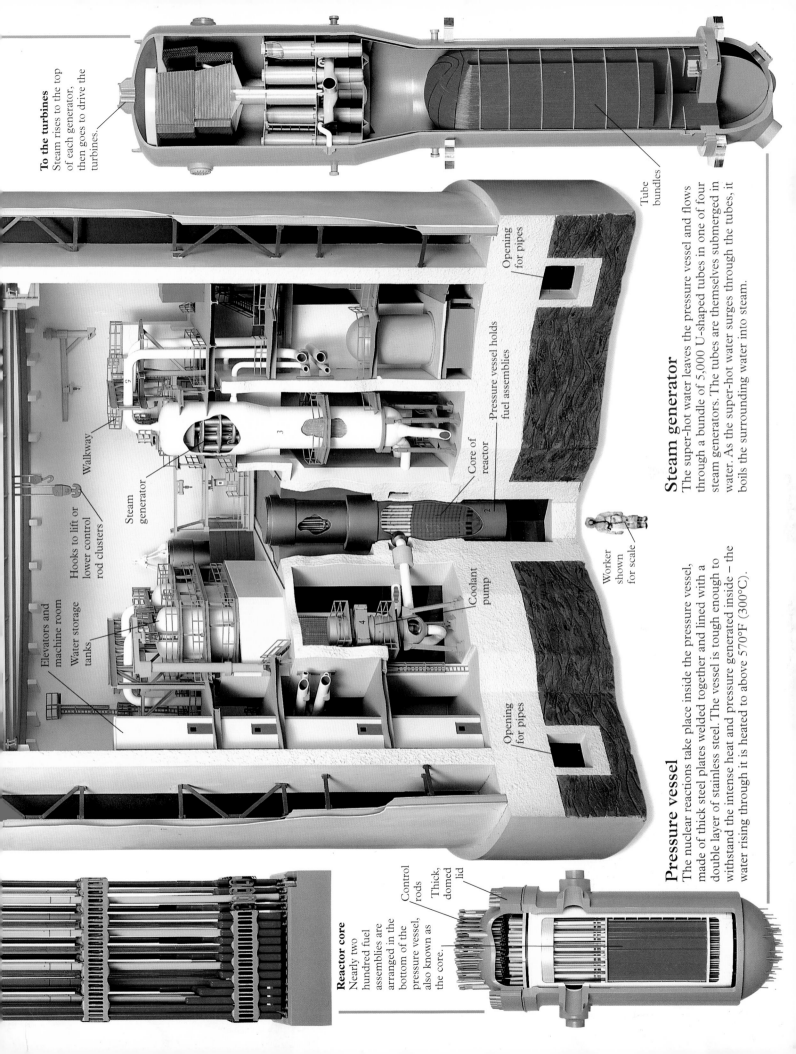

To the turbines
Steam rises to the top of each generator, then goes to drive the turbines.

Tube bundles

Steam generator
The super-hot water leaves the pressure vessel and flows through a bundle of 5,000 U-shaped tubes in one of four steam generators. The tubes are themselves submerged in water. As the super-hot water surges through the tubes, it boils the surrounding water into steam.

Opening for pipes

Walkway

Steam generator

Hooks to lift or lower control rod clusters

Elevators and machine room

Water storage tanks

Core of reactor

Pressure vessel holds fuel assemblies

Coolant pump

Worker shown for scale

Opening for pipes

Pressure vessel
The nuclear reactions take place inside the pressure vessel, made of thick steel plates welded together and lined with a double layer of stainless steel. The vessel is tough enough to withstand the intense heat and pressure generated inside – the water rising through it is heated to above 570°F (300°C).

Reactor core
Nearly two hundred fuel assemblies are arranged in the bottom of the pressure vessel, also known as the core.

Control rods

Thick, domed lid

Drill floor

Drilling derrick

Helideck

Crew quarters
More than 100 crew members live in this module.

211/19 C.B.G. MURCHISON

Lifeboat

Water pump
These pumps stand ready in case of a fire.

Home at sea
The accommodation module houses living quarters, a kitchen, a dining room, recreation area, and training area.

Seabed city

Drilling for oil at sea is difficult and dangerous. The drilling equipment weighs several tons, and it has to be taken out to sea and supported on a platform hundreds of feet above the seabed – suffering frequent stormy weather. Many oil rigs, like the Murchison platform in the North Sea, are anchored to the sea bottom. A tall steel frame called a jacket is built onshore, carried out to sea on a barge, then upended and attached to the seabed. The derrick and all the other machinery needed to extract the oil are built on a platform on top of the jacket. Then the task of drilling the wells begins. Like a city at sea, people live on the platform and work in shifts to run the drill, pumps, power plant, and control room.

Oil tanks
Before it is pumped ashore, oil is kept here.

Mud stores
The chemical mix, called mud, used to cool the drill bit, is stored here.

Workshop
Repair jobs are carried out in the workshop.

Storage at sea
Much of the platform is set aside for storing equipment and supplies, from barrels of crude oil to bottles of cooking oil.

Steel towers
The upper part of the rig was made in separate sections, or modules, each designed for a specific task. The modules were brought out to sea on barges and lifted into place on top of the jacket.

Derrick
The tallest part of the rig, the drilling derrick, provides support for the drilling equipment.

Radio control room

Valves
These regulate the flow of oil.

Gas burner
Where there is oil, there is usually natural gas, so most oil rigs also produce some gas. Some powers machinery on the rig. The excess is burned off at the flare boom, a metal arm that sticks out to one side.

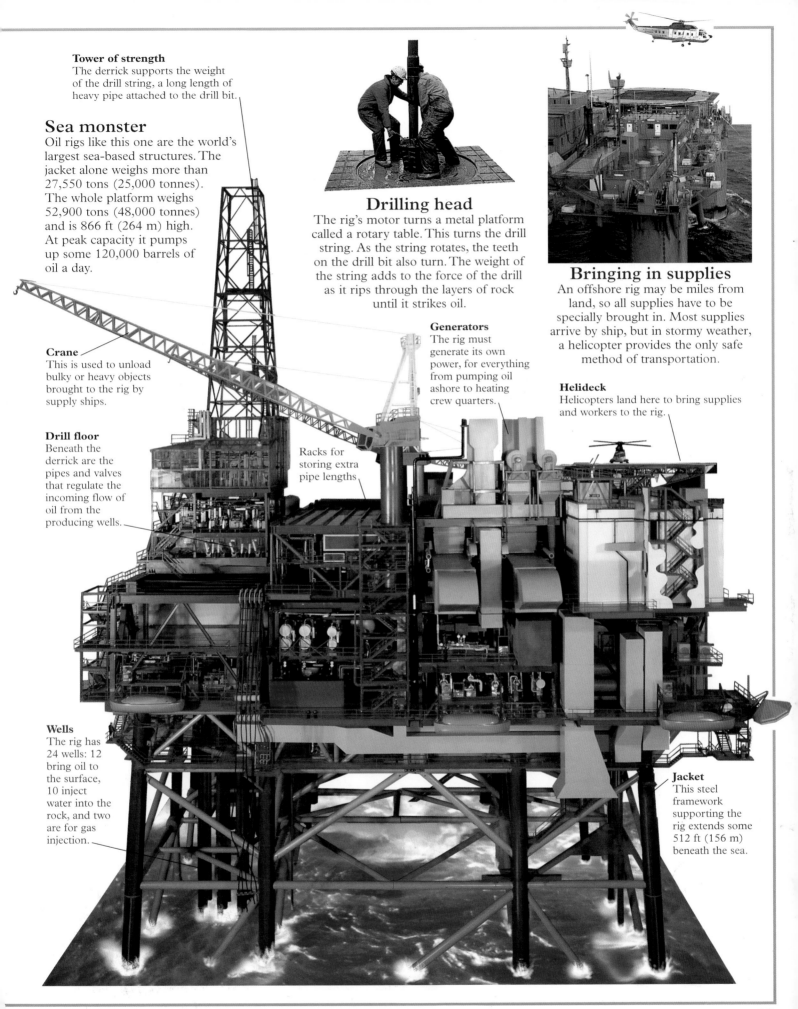

Tower of strength
The derrick supports the weight of the drill string, a long length of heavy pipe attached to the drill bit.

Sea monster
Oil rigs like this one are the world's largest sea-based structures. The jacket alone weighs more than 27,550 tons (25,000 tonnes). The whole platform weighs 52,900 tons (48,000 tonnes) and is 866 ft (264 m) high. At peak capacity it pumps up some 120,000 barrels of oil a day.

Drilling head
The rig's motor turns a metal platform called a rotary table. This turns the drill string. As the string rotates, the teeth on the drill bit also turn. The weight of the string adds to the force of the drill as it rips through the layers of rock until it strikes oil.

Bringing in supplies
An offshore rig may be miles from land, so all supplies have to be specially brought in. Most supplies arrive by ship, but in stormy weather, a helicopter provides the only safe method of transportation.

Crane
This is used to unload bulky or heavy objects brought to the rig by supply ships.

Generators
The rig must generate its own power, for everything from pumping oil ashore to heating crew quarters.

Helideck
Helicopters land here to bring supplies and workers to the rig.

Drill floor
Beneath the derrick are the pipes and valves that regulate the incoming flow of oil from the producing wells.

Racks for storing extra pipe lengths

Wells
The rig has 24 wells: 12 bring oil to the surface, 10 inject water into the rock, and two are for gas injection.

Jacket
This steel framework supporting the rig extends some 512 ft (156 m) beneath the sea.

Service at sea

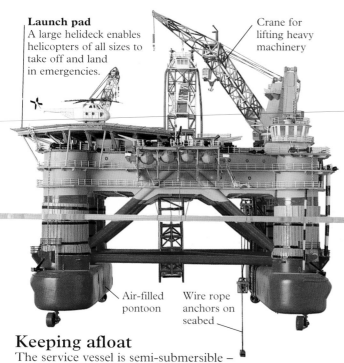

Launch pad
A large helideck enables helicopters of all sizes to take off and land in emergencies.

Crane for lifting heavy machinery

When a building needs repairs, it is usually easy to get to the part that needs fixing. Cranes, scaffolding, and cradles suspended from the roof take painters, maintenance workers, and even window cleaners where they need to go. If there is a fire, fire engines with ladders and booms provide quick access. But what happens with a vast oil rig anchored to the seabed? Some of the work has to be done underwater; other jobs are carried out high up on the rig, often in howling gales. This service vessel, used both for underwater and topside operations, provides the ultimate in service at sea. Like a huge floating repair shop, it helps with all the operations required on a rig, from routine inspection and basic repairs, to fighting fires and coping with blowouts and other emergencies.

Air-filled pontoon

Wire rope anchors on seabed

Keeping afloat
The service vessel is semi-submersible – it floats above the water on round, air-filled "feet" called pontoons. The massive columns that support the decks rise from a pair of pontoons. The vessel is powered by nine enormous diesel engines. When it arrives at the rig, it is moored in position using up to eight anchors on tough wire ropes.

Triple decker
The two lower decks of the vessel provide accommodations for 128 people, from rig maintenance workers and safety inspectors to firefighters and deep-sea divers.

Control room
A wall of windows all around gives the control room crew a view across a wide area.

Access tower
To reach different parts of the rig, the tower can turn horizontally through a wide angle of 135 degrees.

Tower provides emergency escape route.

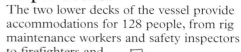

Signal flags

Crane hook

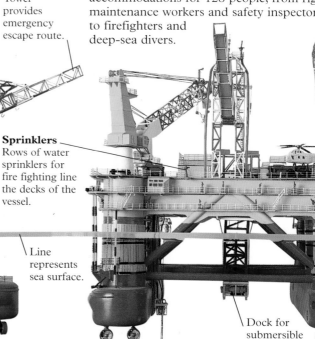

Sprinklers
Rows of water sprinklers for fire fighting line the decks of the vessel.

Line represents sea surface.

Dock for submersible

Emergency access
A large 121-ft (37-m) long access tower can swing out over the top of an oil rig. This enables fire-fighting teams to get on to the rig quickly – and the crew to get off the rig quickly in an emergency.

Submersible is docked beneath the service vessel.

Submersible
Some parts of an oil rig stretch down hundreds of feet to the seabed. People in scuba gear or diving suits cannot go this deep, so a special submersible is used for deep diving.

Fire practice

One of the most crucial tasks of the service vessel is to bring firefighters and their equipment to a rig. Emergency drills like this one keep the fire-fighting team in practice.

Jets in action

If there is a fire or blowout (when a drill bit hits a pocket of pressurized oil or gas) on an oil rig, the service vessel saturates the well head with water. It sprays from 16 jets called fire monitors mounted on its decks, delivering up to 40,000 gallons (151,414 liters) of water per minute.

Divers at work

Much of the inspection and routine maintenance of an oil rig's supporting jacket is done by divers. This diver wears a special helmet that gives protection from pressure and ocean currents.

Observation tower
This tower supports an observation post as well as communication equipment.

Helicopter on helipad

Access to helipad

Load lifter
The crane with the shorter jib can lift weights of up to 55 tons (50 tonnes).

Support pillars
The enormous pillars that hold up the decks are made of timber-clad steel.

Propeller
Six propellers help power the vessel.

Pontoon
Rounded metal pontoons keep the vessel afloat.

All-purpose platform

Although it is well-equipped for emergencies, the service vessel is mostly used for routine work. Its three cranes can load heavy items onto a rig, while its diving facilities are invaluable for joining the under-sea pipelines that connect rigs to the shore.

Glossary

A

Aerodynamic Term used to describe a structure designed so that air will pass over it with minimal resistance, so reducing wind load on the structure.

Airfoil Structure designed in a similar way to the cross-section of an airplane wing.

Pont de Normandie, France

Archaeology The study of the material remains of past human cultures.

Architecture The art and science of designing buildings and supervising their construction.

Atrium Tall internal space in a building with a glass roof to let in natural light.

Submersible housed under oil platform

B

Ballast Material used to weigh a structure down, preventing uplift due to wind or water pressure.

Boring machine Mechanism used to excavate a tunnel or other underground structure; often called a tunnel-boring machine (TBM).

C

Cable sheath Protective covering surrounding cables on a bridge.

Cantilever bridge Type of bridge in which fixed arms stretch outward from anchored piers to support a central span.

Centripetal force
Force that acts inward on a body traveling along a curved path.

Cladding Weatherproof "skin" covering the outside walls of a building.

Cofferdam Structure made of concrete-filled tubes or similar elements, designed to keep water out of the foundations of such structures as bridge piers.

Computer-aided design The use of computers in the design of buildings and other structures; often abbreviated as CAD.

Cross-braces Diagonal members inserted in a rectangular frame to make it more rigid.

Fuel assembly of a nuclear reactor

D

Damper cable Cable fitted between parts of a cable-stayed bridge to reduce vibration.

Deck The floor of a bridge, running between the piers and carrying the roadway or railroad line.

Derrick Towerlike framework over an oil well that allows drill tubes to be lowered and lifted.

Drill string Pipe that stretches down from an oil rig to the oil-bearing rock below; oil flows up the pipe and the lower end holds the drill bit.

Duct Channel or tube designed to contain wiring or other services, or to allow air flow.

E

Engineering The profession of applying scientific principles to the design and construction of buildings and structures.

F

Fiber-optic cable Cable made of very thin flexible fibers of glass, used to transmit data.

Fly tower Tall structure above the stage of a theater, enabling scenery and other items to be lowered (or "flown") onto the stage.

G

Gantry A kind of framework used to support a moving overhead crane or similar mechanism.

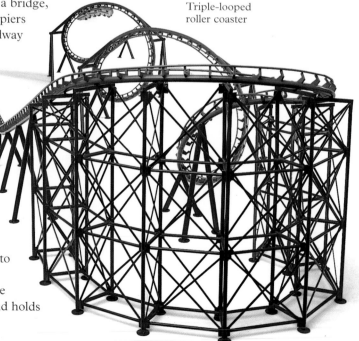

Triple-looped roller coaster

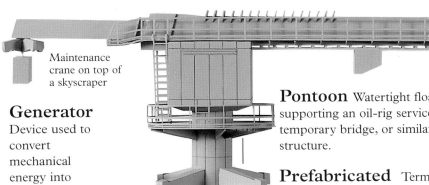

Maintenance crane on top of a skyscraper

Generator
Device used to convert mechanical energy into electricity.

J

Jack Device for raising a heavy object such as a motor vehicle or part of a building.

Jacket Framework that supports an oil rig on the seabed.

Worker inside service tunnel

M

Maintenance The routine tasks, such as cleaning, painting, and replacing worn parts, needed to keep a structure in good condition.

Mobile crane Crane that can be moved along a track or on a truck to the required position.

P

Pier Short wall designed to bear a heavy load, such as an arch.

Pillar An upright structure of stone, brick, or metal that holds up part of a building or other structure.

Pontoon Watertight float supporting an oil-rig service vessel, temporary bridge, or similar structure.

Prefabricated Term used to describe parts of a structure that are manufactured off-site, then moved to the building site where they can be assembled quickly.

Pylon Tall, upright structure to which the cables on a cable-stayed bridge are attached.

R

Reactor Short for nuclear reactor; the incredibly strong container in which the chemical reactions in a nuclear power station take place.

Reinforced concrete A type of specially strengthened concrete with steel bars or mesh embedded inside it.

S

Sill Horizontal ledge below a window or the lowest horizontal part of a frame.

Skyscraper Tall, multistory building, the weight of which is supported by a metal framework.

Span Distance between the supports of a bridge or arch.

Spoil Rock and other waste material dug up in an excavation.

Structure Name for any complex construction.

Suspension bridge Bridge in which the deck is hung from ropes or cables passing over twin towers.

T

Terminal In an airport, a building for arrivals and departures.

Topside Upper part of an oil rig or service vessel, above the water level.

Truss Structural framework used to support a roof or bridge.

Eurostar auto-carrying car

Turbine Machine with a bladed rotor that turns to convert the energy of a moving fluid into mechanical energy.

V

Valve Device that turns on or off, or controls, the flow of a liquid or gas.

Ventilation System that provides control over the air quality in a building by removing stale air and allowing fresh air to come in.

Viaduct Bridge with many spans carrying a road or railroad, often across a valley.

W

Welding Attaching two pieces of metal or plastic by softening them with heat.

Reactor pressure vessel

Index

Acknowledgments

Design assistance:
Rachael Dyson, Iain Morris, Emma Bowden, Salesh Patel, and Jason Gonzalez

Photoshop retouching:
Bob Warner

Illustrations:
John Woodcock

Thanks to:
Gary Ombler for photographic assistance, Nicky Studdart for DTP design, Nicola Waine for editorial assistance, Neville Graham for design guidance in the early stages of the book, and Marion Dent for the index.

DK would also like to thank Donald and Arthur Smith of Donald Smith Modelmakers for their kind permission to photograph their model of the service vessel and the oil platform, the Aberdeen Maritime Museum, the staff of the Thames Barrier Visitor's Center, the staff of the Sizewell B Press Office, Katy Harris of Sir Norman Foster and Partners, Sylvia Jones at the Eurotunnel Exhibition Centre, John Staunton and John Loader at Ove Arup and Partners, Robert Marshall at Barton Myers Associates, Roderick Coyne and Francis Graves at Alsop & Störmer Architects, M. Nicolas Fritz of the Department of Architecture and Building in Marseille, Clare Endicott at Michael Hopkins & Partners, Chigusa Oshima at Kansai International Airport Co., Ltd., and Shunji Ishida and Isabella Carpiceci at the Renzo Piano Building Workshop.

Picture credits
r=right, l=left, t=top, c=center, b=below, a=above.

Alsop and Störmer: 16tr, 17tl, 17tr; **Ancient Art and Architecture:** 18tr; **British Gas Plc:** 19tr; **Mary Evans Picture Library:** 10cr, 11r, 20cr, 24cr, 30tr, 34tr, 36tr; **Sir Norman Foster and Partners:** 10 ar, 10cr, 11cr, 12al; **Dennis Gilbert:** 9tl, 32cl, 32c; **Robert Harding Picture Library:** 20tr, 24tr, 29tr; **Michael Hopkins and Parnters:** 8b, 9tr, 9b; **The Image Bank:** 25c, Gary Gladstone 35tc; **Kansai International Airport Co. Ltd.:** 32tr; **Ian Lambot:** 12tl, 12br, 12tr, 13l, 13b, 13r; **Frank Lane Picture Agency:** 25cr; **Magnum Photos Limited:** 27tr, Jean Gaumy 27tc; **Barton Myers Associates:** 14bl, 15tl, 15tr; **Popperfoto:** 11c, 28tr, 33cr;

QA Photos Ltd: 20cl, 20c, 22tl, 23br; **Renzo Piano Building Workshop:** 8cl, 8cr; **Rex Features:** 19cr, 30c, 32cr, 35cl, 38bl, 41tl, /Berry Bingel 39tr, /Kiry O'Donnel 18tr,/Sipa 30bl, /Sipa/Marais Gaussen 12cl, /Andrew Testa 31tl, /The Times 36tr, /Mike Toy 41tr; **Science Photo Library:** 36br, 37bc, /Martin Bond 25cl, /Richard Folwell 41tc, /David Parker 8cr; **Thames Barrier:** 29tl; **Thames Water Utilities Limited:** 18bl,18c; **Unichrome Bath Limited:** 29br; **Zefa Pictures:** 39tc

Every effort has been made to trace the copyright holders. DK apologizes for any unintentional omissions and would be pleased, in such cases, to add an acknowledgment in future editions.